Dancing Wheels

Dancing Wheels

Patricia McMahon

Illustrated with photographs by John Godt

Houghton Mifflin Company ☼ Boston 2000

ACKNOWLEDGMENTS

First and foremost, I must thank Diana Moilanen, librarian and dancer, who spoke to me that day in Cleveland, telling me of a book I should write. And yes, you were you right.

I am deeply indebted to all those associated with Dancing Wheels for the warmth of their welcome and their great kindness in allowing me to attend their workshops, rehearsals, and performances. I must particularly thank:

Mary Verdi-Fletcher for graciously answering all my questions and for the generosity of her insights, the openness of her answers. She is simply extraordinary.

Barbara and Sabatino Verlezza for allowing a stranger to come along, for including me every day in every way, and for allowing me to dance the "Tammorriata."

And Nancy Lushington, as well.

All the young dancers of the week's workshop, in particular Sabatino the younger and Jessica Taylor, whose mother showed me the way.

And of course, Jenny Sikora and Devin Alberda, who are two fine dancers, and two swell (big) kids. I thank them for allowing me into their lives and their dancing.

I must thank the Sikora and Alberda families for adding our work and needs to the business of their lives.

Barbara Barstow and Jo Crabtree, librarians extraordinaire, were good friends and companions while I was in Cleveland. A red convertible, a disc jockey, and Janis Joplin on the radio!

Thank you, Sarah and Colin Alexander, for lending me your house while I was in town. You are two more swell kids.

As always, friends keep the home fires burning and make the work possible. So thanks to the Houston contingent—particularly Laura Cook and Timmy Cook—and also to Brian Quinn, Alison Quinn, Charley Beall, Andrew and Jennifer Nix, Michael Sims, Jay Mathur, Andreas Bernard, Joseph Beijani, Reece Dukes, Ryan Heuman, Zachary and Alexa West, and of course, their pal, my red-haired guy, Conor Clarke McCarthy, who makes all things possible.

The text of this book is set in Celeste (FontShop).
Book design by Lisa Diercks

Library of Congress Cataloging-in-Publication Data
McMahon, Patricia.
Dancing Wheels / by Patricia McMahon ; illustrated with photographs by John Godt.
p. cm.
ISBN 0-395-88889-1
1. Dance for handicapped children—Juvenile literature. 2. Dance for children—Juvenile literature. 3. Dancing Wheels (Dance group)—Juvenile literature. I. Godt, John, ill. II. Title.
GV1799.2.M36 2000
99-087715

Printed in Singapore
TWP 10 9 8 7 6 5 4 3 2 1

To Claire Guan Yu McCarthy,

who has joined our merry dance,

and

to my aunt, Helen McMullin,

for all she has done for me, especially my first ballet,

that Saturday afternoon in New York

— P. M.

To Diane Roberto

— J. G.

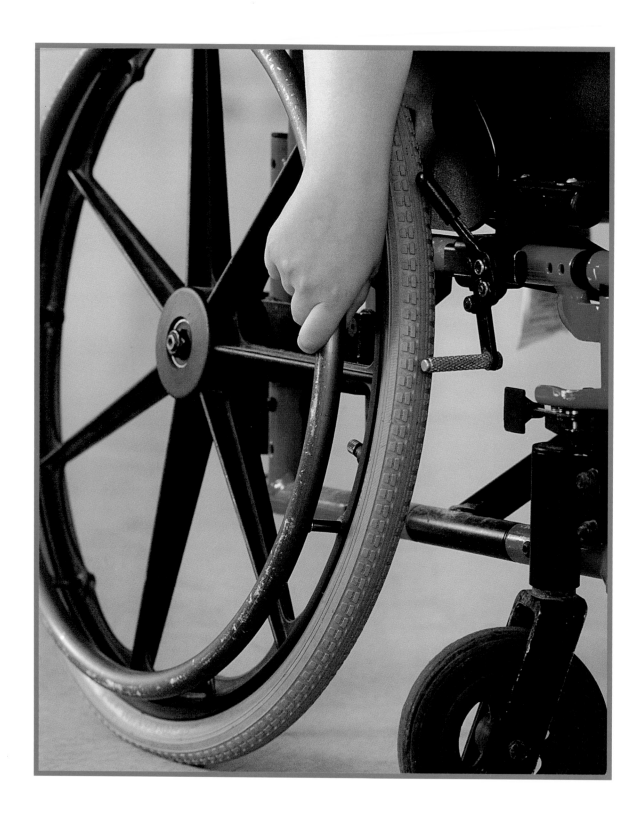

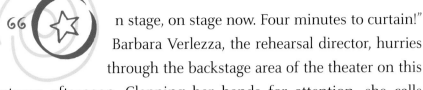 "n stage, on stage now. Four minutes to curtain!" Barbara Verlezza, the rehearsal director, hurries through the backstage area of the theater on this autumn afternoon. Clapping her hands for attention, she calls again, "Everyone to center stage!"

A dancer named Jenny calls out, "Me first," as she rushes to the stage. She is followed by her friend Devin, who asks one last time if he can please, just this once, dance in something besides tights.

"There are kids from my school out there!" he says to no one in particular.

Dancers finish their makeup and rush onto the stage in their costumes, scurrying, wheeling to join the others before the performance begins. They gather in a circle. On the other side of the massive curtain, the audience waits, fidgeting as the lights dim.

Before the performance, Jessica puts on her makeup.

The dancers gather onstage to wish one another well.

"Dancers always believe that all would be well if there were just one more day for rehearsal," Barbara reminds everyone. "But there never is just one more day. We've got to be ready now." The dancers grab one another's hands, reaching down, reaching up. Without words, they wish one another well.

The young dancers follow Sabatino as he leads them through the "Carneval."

Moments later, when everyone is offstage, the curtain goes up, the spotlight comes on. The stand-up dancers walk on, the sit-down dancers wheel on. They pause, pose. The loud, rhythmic sounds of an ancient Italian song fill the air. The dancers move to the music, with the music.

Dancing Wheels takes the stage.

In the center of the whirling and the twirling, Sabatino Verlezza and Mary Verdi-Fletcher dance together. They are the leaders of the company. Sabatino, a stand-up dancer and choreographer, creates the dances for the group. And Mary? Mary Verdi-Fletcher is the reason everyone is here today, the reason for the dancing. Because for years Mary had a dream, an idea everyone thought was crazy.

*M*ary Verdi-Fletcher was born with spina bifida, a spinal cord problem that occurs before birth, while a baby is growing. Spina bifida creates a weakness in the legs and spine and often prevents feeling or muscle control in the lower portion of the body. When Mary was born in the 1950s, a baby with her condition was not expected to live long or to have a normal life. But the doctors who made that prediction had not understood Mary's family. The doctors were so very wrong about Mary's life.

Mary, who always knew she wanted to be a dancer, helps show others the way.

Mary's parents did not leave her in the hospital; they took her home. They had braces made for her legs to help her walk. Mary was not shut out of their world, she was part of it. When her cousins and friends danced and played around the house, Mary found her own way to join in. Mary's parents told her not to think of what she couldn't do but of what she could do.

An interpreter translates in sign language while Mary addresses the audience.

Yet even her parents never imagined that what Mary would want to do was dance. They never imagined this theater filled with applause—all because of her.

Mary wheels off to watch in the wings as the next dance begins. Sabatino, playing the jester, leads the children of Dancing Wheels on a merry dance. Devin, a stand-up dancer, partners with Jenny, a sit-down dancer. The smallest dancer, little Sabatino—who shares his father's name—hurries along throughout the dance. Mary smiles, watching him catch up to the others.

When she was small, Mary was always hurrying to catch up. And she did. When she was older and everyone began disco dancing, so did Mary. She and a friend entered a dance contest. They won first prize along with everyone's cheers. Mary knew for sure that this was what she wanted to do, this was what she wanted to be: a dancer.

Mary entered more contests, won more prizes. She looked for dancers to teach her. She studied and worked hard. She did not listen to people who said, "You cannot dance if you are in a wheelchair." She did not listen to people who said, "If you dance in a chair, it is not really dancing." She did not listen when people said, "Wheelchair dancers should only dance with others in wheelchairs."

Mary formed her own company, Dancing Wheels. The company has two kinds of dancers: stand-up dancers who use their legs, arms, backs, necks, and faces for expression; and sit-down dancers who use their legs, arms, backs, necks, and faces for expression — along with their wheelchairs.

Mary watches the young dancers rush offstage. Devin and Jenny hurry to change their costumes. They have lead roles in the main dance on today's program. Jenny almost barrels into three people, calling out "Sorry! Sorry!" as she whips by. Devin complains again about wearing tights today. Little Sabatino hitches a ride on a sit-down dancer's chair.

Young Sabatino came to live in Cleveland when Mary invited his parents to work with her and the Dancing Wheels company. She thought they were the right people to keep her crazy idea going. So the Verlezzas came.

Sabatino is a dancer like his parents.

*With lights,
costumes, makeup,
music, and
movement, the
dancers perform.*

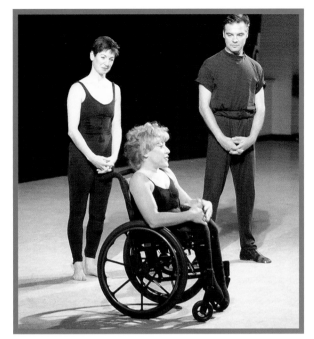

Barbara, Mary, and Sabatino dance, work, and teach together.

Mary and the grown-up Sabatino run Dancing Wheels together, and they dance together as partners. Barbara oversees rehearsals, and she dances with the company as well. Dancing Wheels travels all over the country, performing and teaching. And Dancing Wheels offers classes for both stand-up and sit-down dancers.

The company is always busy—learning new dances, practicing moves, and rehearsing for performances. The studio is the place where the dancers practice—over and over again—until the dances are perfect, or as perfect as they can be. And the studio is the place where individual dancers become a company, two dancers become partners, two partners become friends.

Devin and Jenny are the partners who open the main dance.

Jenny and Devin are partners both in the studio and on the stage.

They rush out of the dressing rooms to wait in the wings by Mary. They are about to begin "The Sorcerer's Apprentices." Jenny fidgets in her wheelchair. *No more time to worry,* she thinks. *Time to begin dancing.* Devin tries to loosen up, moving his legs, reminding himself of his opening moves. He wonders if Jenny is running through the dance in her mind, the way he does. The dance is a long one, but Devin feels ready. He has done this dance before. And he and Jenny worked hard this summer, getting ready for performances like this.

During the summer, Dancing Wheels holds workshops for dancers. Jenny Sikora and Devin Alberda, along with Devin's sister, Kristen, and several other dancers who are onstage today, were part of those workshops. There were others in the workshops who may never have danced before. They all studied and worked together under Barbara and Sabatino. It was hard work, Devin remembers. All day, every day, a group of young people came together to dance in the studio.

During a summer workshop, stand-up and sit-down dancers work and rehearse together.

Amara listens to a friend, while little Sabatino enjoys the dance.

n the first morning of a workshop, dancers are scattered around the high-ceilinged, brightly lit studio. Jenny zips in and out, looking for Devin. On the fly, she passes two girls she doesn't know sitting quietly by the door in their wheelchairs. Devin arrives with Kristen and their good friend Jessica. Sabatino waves some dancers in as his son runs over to Jenny and Devin. "I've got a funny story to tell you about a bird," the younger Sabatino begins, but he is interrupted by his mother, who sends him on an errand.

"I've just got to tell you what happened," Jenny says to Devin.

Lore joins the circle of dancers.

Since they live on opposite sides of the city, the dance studio is where Jenny and Devin get to meet.

"Dancers," Barbara calls out, interrupting Jenny as well, "Dancers, please join the circle." Jenny and Devin rush to their places. A girl in blue waits until Mark, another dancer, uses his hands to tell her what was said. The two girls in the chairs by the door sit waiting.

"Dancers, please!" With a wide gesture of his arm, Sabatino motions to the two girls. Katie, the one with the ponytail, looks over her shoulder to see which dancers he means, but she finds no one behind her.

"Dancers, over here." Sabatino invites them to the circle. Exchanging worried looks, Katie and Amara join the group. Jenny and Devin move over to make room for the two girls.

"We need to learn each other's names," Sabatino explains. "We will do this through movement, for dance is movement. Everyone,

Mark translates Barbara's spoken words into sign language for Lore.

listen to the sound of your name. Listen to the rhythm of your name, the song of your name."

Then he shows them how, sounding out his name, "SAH-BAA-TEE-NO." He turns the sounds into a small song. Moving his hands and arms to the sound, Sabatino dances his name.

"Everyone try," he urges.

Mark goes next. He is the translator for Lore, the girl in blue who isn't able to hear. When Sabatino or Barbara speaks, Mark signs the words for Lore. To dance his name, he puts his hands out with closed fists, then turns them over quickly, palms wide. "MARK."

Devin laughs and breaks his name into two syllables. Turning his head side to side, he bends his arms like a character painted on the inside wall of a pyramid. He moves his arms in and out. *Dance like an Egyptian,* he thinks.

Jenny stretches her name out, her arms up in the air, two jets flying. "JEEEENNNNYYYY." Devin thinks this sounds just like Jenny rushing in and out of places, a jet zooming to get somewhere.

So they go around the circle, repeating each name, feeling silly or acting silly, adding dances for the names Kristen, Jessica, Jennifer, Nancy, Katie who wasn't sure she was a dancer, Amara, and little Sabatino.

Lore lifts her toe to her nose and down. Sabatino jumps in and says, "If you can lift your leg, do it. If you cannot lift your leg, lift your hand. Echo the motion." So they go, until all of them have danced their names.

T he dancers form lines and face the mirrors. Devin and Jenny are in different lines. The sit-downs take places behind the stand-ups; then the stand-ups sit down on the floor. "We're going to work those muscles now," Sabatino warns them. He calls out directions, his words a song.

> *Flex your hands, flex your feet.*
> *Fold like a book. Open like a book.*
> *You are the book. This is your story.*

The experienced dancers move along with him. The dancers who are new frown with concentration, following as well as they

Stretching and reaching, the dancers follow Sabatino's lead.

can. Lore follows Sabatino's movements in the mirror, not his words in the air. Bodies fold, open again.

"This is about what you *can* do, not what you cannot," Sabatino says to encourage them. Mary, opening and folding with everyone else, hears the same words her parents said, the words that led her to be here this morning in this studio.

"Do it as best you can," Sabatino says. Wanting them to sit tall, he tells everyone, "Imagine you are sitting in a pool of water up to your nose. Now rise out of the water. Come on, Devin, you are going under."

Devin pulls himself up.

"Good," Sabatino urges. "But," he adds, "can you stay like that all day?"

Eleven-year-old Devin is at home in the studio.

Devin works hard on holding the position, trying not to join in the laughter around him. Dancing is Devin's great joy. His favorite T-shirt says: WILL DANCE FOR FOOD. Having begun dancing with the School of the Cleveland Ballet, Devin and Kristen started to

Devin's shirt says it all.

study with Dancing Wheels after their mother heard about the group. Like the sit-down dancers, their mother uses a wheelchair to get around. Devin plans on becoming a ballet dancer. But unlike so many of the dancers, who are proud to have everyone know about their work, Devin sometimes feels he has to be quiet, to keep his plans to himself. Some of the boys his age make fun of dancing. They make fun of dancers, especially male dancers. And they make fun of Devin. But here in the studio it doesn't matter. Here in the studio, Devin has no problems with dancing, unless he doesn't work hard enough.

Barbara wanders through the studio while Sabatino calls out the

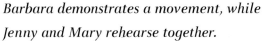
Barbara demonstrates a movement, while
Jenny and Mary rehearse together.

movements. She corrects positions, helps new dancers, and encourages everyone. "Pretend you have two beach balls under your arms," she suggests to Jenny. "Hold them carefully, but not too tight."

Jenny tries carefully to hold the beach balls that are not there. "That was well done," Sabatino declares. "Now let's try it again, only may I suggest you try breathing this time?" The dancers cannot help but breathe as they burst out laughing.

Jenny laughs the hardest, dropping her imaginary beach balls. Jenny loves to be silly and is happy to be so at the slightest invitation. When Sabatino gives her the stop-being-too-silly look, Jenny takes a breath and picks up the movement. Jenny loves to

Jenny, who has been dancing seven years, works on her movements.

be at the Dancing Wheels studio as much as she loves to be goofy. Jenny's parents first brought her to a dance class there after seeing Mary dance. Jenny was four years old, the same age Mary was when she first told someone she wanted to be a dancer. Like Mary, Jenny was born with spina bifida. Like Mary, Jenny used crutches to get around when she was younger. Now Jenny uses her fast-flying wheelchair. While her classmates may have to dodge Jenny's chair, they are relieved that she no longer uses her crutches to trip other kids on the playground.

As she watches Devin warming up, Jenny knows she is lucky. She doesn't have to worry about kids making fun of her because she dances. A lot of kids in her school think it's great that Jenny gets her picture in the paper or is interviewed by reporters. Jenny knows, though, that some kids say mean things about her being in a wheelchair. It hurts her feelings, right down to her bones, just as Devin's feelings are hurt by the boys who make fun of his dancing. But when Jenny and Devin come to the studio, they can simply be themselves. At the studio, it doesn't matter what anyone else thinks. Here dancers dance, whether or not some people say boys shouldn't dance or girls in wheelchairs can't.

"Now dig with your arms," Sabatino calls out.

"Dig as if the air were made of money," Barbara suggests. Jenny and Devin and the other dancers reach up, trying to catch as much money as they can. Each one has his or her own idea of how to spend it.

After floor exercises, the dancers practice moving across the studio, using the space as they would a stage.

"Your movements must be big," the teachers remind them. "So the audience can see them." Dancers are always being reminded of the audience, even when the audience is not there. Devin and Jenny imagine the audience that will come see them this fall when

Arms soar into the air as the dancers practice movement.

Dancing Wheels performs "The Sorcerer's Apprentices."

The stand-ups go to one side of the room, the sit-downs to the other. Jenny wants to dance with her friends. She contents herself with making faces at them from her side of the room. The stand-ups then prance across the floor.

"In rhythm," Barbara calls out. "Without rhythm there is no dance. And remember, it doesn't matter if you do it wrong, as long as you do it big."

Leaping arms follow Sabatino as Barbara leads leaping legs.

"Wheelers, after me," Sabatino calls out. "Leaping arms, I want leaping arms." The groups pass on the floor. Lore cannot stop laughing. Amara and Katie struggle on the turns. Jenny zips through them easily. "And again," Sabatino calls. Like two armies, they march past one another.

Young Sabatino, Devin, Jessica, Kristen, and Jennifer share Jenny's joke at lunchtime.

And though it seems they have only been there a few minutes, it has been hours. "Lunch break!" Sabatino calls.

"I'm first!" Jenny declares as she races to the door. No one catches up to her.

"A parrot sat on my head yesterday," little Sabatino tells his friends at lunch.

"You're crazy," Jenny tells him. "Want to play see-food?" she asks, ready to open her full mouth. Today nobody falls for her joke.

ll afternoon, the dancers work and practice together. "It is essential to be able to dance well *with* someone," Sabatino tells them. "Dance cannot always be done alone."

"Try to think of it as a series of questions and answers," Mary suggests. "One dancer's movement asks a question; the other's movement answers the question. Learn to trust the other dancer."

Barbara and Katie
work on becoming
partners. Devin and
Jenny already are.

Barbara grabs Katie to demonstrate, and she leans back against her. Katie does not let her fall. Katie breaks into a smile. Jenny and Devin try it, too. They have been partners for several years now. Jenny thinks they have been asking the question, "Will you be my friend?" and answering each other, "Yes!"

And so it goes each day of the workshop. Long mornings and afternoons of work. The new dancers learn different ways to think of their bodies and their movements. The others practice the steps they know and try to improve.

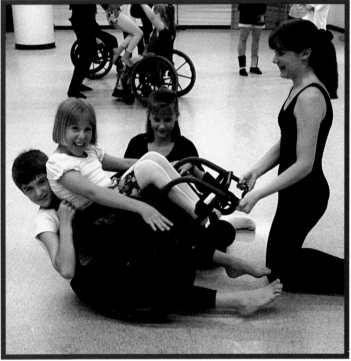

Jenny, Devin, Kristen, and Jessica improvise a dance on Jenny's chair.

One time Barbara breaks the dancers into groups. The studio becomes quiet except for the sound of feet and wheels on the floor. Each group tries out movements, improvising. They ask questions, receive answers, and connect the movements into a dance.

Jenny, Devin, Kristen, and Jessica work as silently as the rest, until they all try balancing in Jenny's chair. Breaking out in loud laughter, they make a shaky structure even shakier. "Look out below!" Mary calls across the studio as they begin to topple. She knows about falling out of chairs. In dance, it happens.

Every morning of the workshop, Sabatino begins with exercises in front of the mirror. "All right, who is sore this morning?" he asks one day. "No one? Well, I'll fix that!"

The patterns of movement begin.

Lift your arm, and two, and three, and four.
Out to the side, and two, and three, and four.
And to the sky, and two, and three, and four.

"Come on, you can do this," Sabatino urges the dancers.

"The body turns here." Sabatino shows them. "Sit-downs, turn your chairs. Does everyone understand?" he asks them. "Say yes, even if you do not." He walks among the dancers, counting out the beat. "Count with me, and two and three and four. Standers, hold your ankles; seateds, hold your chairs. Now lift your chests high," he urges. "Come on, we're taking a picture for Grandma."

Devin lifts his chest high, feels the soreness he wouldn't admit was there. Feels it in his legs as well. Yesterday, after class, when his mother asked him to water the lawn, Devin sprayed himself as well, cooling off from a long day of dance. Then, for good measure, he sprayed Kristen, who tried to get him back. Their water fight turned into a dance, a brother-and-sister water dance. They ended up leaping around the garden. Devin sees dance everywhere, catches himself making movements he knows he could expand. He thinks he might someday create dances, like Sabatino.

Kristen and Devin dance in their own backyard.

The stand-up dancers take the floor in front of the sit-downs.

"Make it bigger," Barbara calls out to them. "Remember the audience in the back row."

Here they are again, Jenny thinks. There's always an audience in a dancer's mind. Like the one Devin hopes will not contain members of his class. And if it does, he does not want to be seen wearing what all dancers wear almost all the time.

He has asked Sabatino if he can wear something else when they do "The Sorcerer's Apprentices." Sabatino tells Devin to stop worrying, that everyone in the audience will not be focused on Devin. But Devin is not convinced.

Jenny knows she doesn't really need to come to the studio or to a performance to have an audience. With five older brothers, one older sister, and three younger brothers, plus two parents, she has a built-in audience at home. At her house, just trying to get everyone into a family picture takes work. Some of her brothers were adopted, like Jenny. And also like Jenny, some have had problems from birth that require braces or wheelchairs or other adjust-

The Sikora family is a ready-made audience.

Jenny, with her brother Timmy, shows off her favorite T-shirt.

ments. But they are all Sikoras now, and there are enough of them to make their own audience. Then again, Jenny realizes, rounding them up to watch her would take all day. Thinking about her parents, Jenny realizes how like Mary's parents they are, and how much of what Sabatino says about dance is in Jenny's family's daily life. *Think about what you* can *do, not about what you can't.* That could be the Sikora family motto.

Jenny leads the group as the wheelers turn sharp on the count of six.

As the workshop continues, the dancers begin to put together the puzzle pieces that make up a whole dance. There is a quick turn in one dance that seems hard for the sit-downs to get right.

"Learn the numbers, wheelers," Sabatino urges them. "One, two, three, and four—faster—and five and SIX!" Sabatino calls out "six" as if it is the biggest, most important number in the world. "Wheelers, turn sharp on six!" Some make it, some do not. Jenny does, starting out across the floor ahead of the others.

The dancers get frustrated. They try again. Sabatino tells them to take a break; he can tell they need it. Charlotte, one of the adult sit-down dancers from the Dancing Wheels company, comes in to meet with Mary. While waiting for Mary, she tells all the young dancers how she went bungee-jumping last weekend. Katie wants to know if she jumped in her wheelchair. Jenny thinks she might try jumping . . . after she finishes setting speed records in her new racing chair.

Jenny is ready to go in her racing chair.

n the last day of the workshop, the dancers invite their families and friends to watch them dance. Katie wears a sparkly outfit and reminds herself to turn sharp on six. Jessica and Kristen do a tango around the room while they are waiting. The dancers show all they have

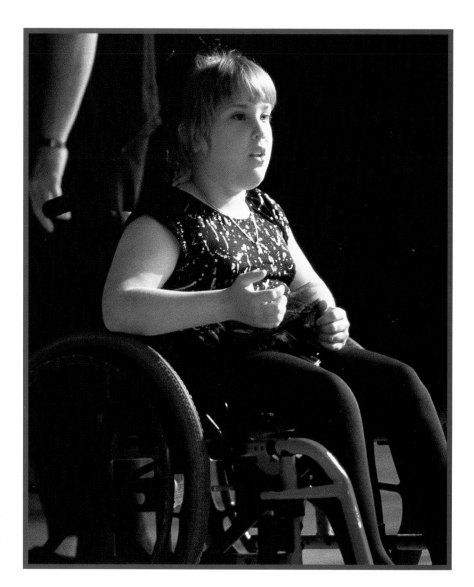

Katie waits for the performance to begin.

done, beginning with floor exercises, moving on to a finished dance. They all join Barbara, Sabatino, and Mary in imitating chickens, lizards, monkeys, and camels. Barbara gets the audience to join in. And to prove that nothing is perfect, Mary's chair flips over during the dance. Barbara and Sabatino act as if that had been the plan. *It doesn't matter if you do it wrong, as long as you do it big!*

After the summer workshop, all the dancers perform.

The puzzle pieces
come together
as a dance.

After the workshop ends, Jenny and Devin carry the skills they have gained over the summer into their fall rehearsals for "The Sorcerer's Apprentices." Devin plays "The Brother Who Can Not See" and Jenny plays "The Sister Who Can Not Walk." Sabatino plays the Sorcerer, who has amazing magical powers. In the opening scene, Devin must carry his friend onto the stage. And she must help him to see. They have to trust each other to be able to make their journey, just as two dancers must trust each other.

In this story, they are trying to reach the Sorcerer's home to become his apprentices. Along the way, they receive special help

Devin and Jenny perform as the Sorcerer's apprentices.

44

*Sabatino the
Sorcerer watches
the magic of his
dance unfold.*

Stand-up and sit-down dancers perform as the Wood Spirits.

from the Wood Spirits. The trees of the forest are transformed and come together to make a chair—a chair for "The Sister Who Can Not Walk." The trees become dancing wheels.

On the day of the performance, Sabatino takes his place on stage, looking exactly as a sorcerer should. The lighting, the costumes, the music are all in place. The practice has been worth it, for the performance comes off without a hitch. Devin forgets about who might be in the audience. He does what he loves to do, and what he does so well. Jenny manages to keep a straight face, count her beats, and dance her best. Mary doesn't fall or fly out of her wheelchair. For much of the performance she sits in the

Sabatino "makes it large" for the audience. Devin and Jenny dance the steps he created.

wings, watching the dance unfurl like magic. All of this is happening today because she didn't listen to what people said she could or couldn't do. She didn't worry about what people would think. She just had a crazy idea . . . she wanted to dance.